I LOVE BANKRUPTCY

HOW IT WORKS AND WHO IT HELPS

I LOVE BANKRUPTCY

DOUG SURPRENANT

TABLE OF CONTENTS

WARNING AND DISCLAIMER

This book is not intended to give legal or tax advice and it does not deal with the technical Federal Rules of Bankruptcy, it is written solely for informational purposes to give the average person some basic knowledge of bankruptcy and to know whether bankruptcy is a good option for them. There are a lot of misconceptions and misbeliefs about bankruptcy so this book is an opportunity to get an idea of how bankruptcy could work for you.

Every attorney has his or her own procedures and experience and this book represents attorney Doug Surprenant's perspective on bankruptcy and how it works. This bias is especially true in the chapters involving loan modifications, debt consolidation, effects on your credit, and the intra-play with divorce where attorney Surprenant speaks from his own experiences and those expressed by his clients.

Remember always seek legal advice regarding your situation, and in each area of concern. Laws change and times change so you must do your own due diligence to ensure correct results. This book is specific to the Commonwealth of Massachusetts and attorney Surprenant makes no representation outside of his geographic practice area which is the eastern District of Massachusetts.

Do not attempt to file bankruptcy on your own; it is wrought with peril.

ABOUT THE AUTHOR

Attorney Doug Surprenant was born in and grew up in Providence RI. He started working for Domino's Pizza as a delivery driver when he was an undergraduate at Brown University. After graduation, he moved to Texas. From there he was promoted and moved eleven times before ending up with his own Domino's franchise in Holbrook MA. In his first year, he won NE Regional Manager of the Year.

After 16 years out of school, Mr. Surprenant decided to change careers and he was admitted into Northeastern School of Law. During school, Mr. Surprenant did three employment related internships and one with a United States bankruptcy judge, William Hillman (now retired). Mr. Surprenant started practicing law in 2005 with a focus on bankruptcy, divorce, and employment law. In addition to his divorce and employment law caseload, attorney Surprenant filed 593 bankruptcies from 2009 to 2019.

Mr. Surprenant or Doug, as he prefers to be called, understands exactly what his clients are going through because he has experienced it himself.

In July 2007, Mr. Surprenant bought a home with no money down, no income verification, and no credit check. He had two mortgages called an 80/20 loan. This represented the questionable practices of the mortgage companies at the time, but like anything that seems too good to be true, it was. Shortly thereafter in 2008, when the mortgage crisis hit, Mr. Surprenant had to close his Domino's Pizza store and he fell behind on his mortgage.

Mr. Surprenant applied for a loan modification in 2009 and after two and a half years of re-submitting documents, he had to file for bankruptcy protection to stop the foreclosure on his home. The mortgage company denied the loan modification five times before he filed a lawsuit in US District court. Attorney Surprenant was able to demonstrate that his mortgage company (the mortgagee) had not followed their own procedures and had lied to him during the modification process. At the summary judgment stage, the judge sided with Mr. Surprenant based on the "totality of the circumstances" and the parties settled.

After receiving his modification, Mr. Surprenant did file for Chapter 13 a second time. With the first mortgage modified, the Chapter 13 allowed him the protection to "cram down" his second mortgage, get a favorable tax repayment plan, and to eliminate both his personal unsecured debt and the business debt incurred by closing his Domino's franchise. Mr. Surprenant is not proud that he filed for bankruptcy, but it did allow him to get a fresh start and to rebuild his finances.

Attorney Surprenant has two adult children, he still lives in his Holbrook home and his current credit score is 718. This is nothing to brag about but, without the bankruptcy, he would not have been able to get his finances under control and move forward as he did.

The sign in Doug's office rings true with so many of his bankruptcy clients:

"I started out with nothing and I have most of it left."

CHAPTER 1
Why I Love Bankruptcy

Almost everyone in financial trouble keeps the stress bottled up inside themselves. They struggle with juggling the bills and "borrowing from Peter to pay Paul." Each week, they must decide how to allocate their money and it can be nerve wracking. It is a game that goes through phases. First you think you have it figured out: increasing your credit balances and or transferring your balances to no interest credit cards. Next, you start paying only the minimums and soon you have no remaining credit.

One client knew the game was over when she mailed in the minimum payment, but the credit card company said that it got there late. So, she was hit with a late charge and the late charge caused the card to go over its limit and so she also got hit with an over the limit charge. She had made a payment of $50 in September, but the balance owed on October's statement had increased by $85.

As a bankruptcy attorney, I see clients on both ends of the spectrum: those who have never missed a payment but must devote their entire paycheck to their bills and those who have simply given up and they just throw the unopened bills into the junk drawer. A great deal of personal debt and its stress is due to credit cards, but the same scenario is true for people struggling with their mortgage and or rent payments. Some people pay the mortgage and nothing else while other people pay the smaller credit card bills and then do not have enough to pay the mortgage on the first of the month. The pressure keeps building and there is no relief in sight.

Many people will openly tell you that their spouse is a jerk, or their kids are lazy, but they will never say, "I cannot afford to buy lunch." AND THIS IS WHY I LOVE BANKRUPTCY because once they speak with me and decide to file, the pressure all goes away. The most common and rewarding statement that I always hear is: "I FINALLY GOT A GOOD NIGHT'S SLEEP."

Bankruptcy is not an easy decision and it should not be taken lightly but it also should not be frowned upon because filing for bankruptcy protection can be a viable, very powerful, and, in some respects, a very easy solution.

I say "an easy solution" but I do not mean an easy way out. The financial struggles and stress along the way and the thousands of dollars that get paid in interest charges is a huge price to pay before you decide to file. If you have any money in the bank, you may get 1% interest if you are lucky, but the credit cards can charge over 28% interest. That is crazy. Whatever you have purchased, you have paid for it many times over.

Bankruptcy is black and white; the rules are extremely clear. Unlike getting divorced or fighting with your neighbor, bankruptcy is straight forward. Your bankruptcy lawyer will ensure that everything you own is protected and if there is a potential problem, then you should know about it before you decide whether to file or not. <u>You can plan for bankruptcy</u>, but you cannot hide anything or be deceitful. So, talk to your attorney and develop a strategy.

In summary, I love bankruptcy because it is straightforward and powerful. It is <u>your decision and your decision alone</u>. You do not need to compromise with an adversary or worry what the judge will do, your lawyer should be able to tell you exactly what will happen. And believe me, when the stress of debt is gone, then you can finally get a good night's sleep.

CHAPTER 2
The Process of Filing Bankruptcy

The first step before you file or even decide if you want to file for bankruptcy protection is to review your situation with a bankruptcy attorney. Each attorney handles the process a little differently but they will have a procedure in place for meeting with you, discussing all your assets and all your liabilities and getting the appropriate paperwork to confirm accuracy and that you are protected.

After you complete the bankruptcy forms with your attorney, then he or she can file your case electronically and you are assigned a docket number and you are known as "the debtor.". Within a day or two after filing your case, a future date will be set up for you to meet with a trustee and this is called a 341 meeting. 341 refers to the section of the bankruptcy code that requires a "meeting of creditors" at which time, the trustee reviews your documents and orally examines the debtor.

You can file for bankruptcy under Chapters 7, 11, 12, or 13. Chapter 7 is known as the liquidation bankruptcy; Chapter 11 is for a reorganization usually involving businesses or wealthy individuals; Chapter 12 is voluntary repayment for family farmers or fisherman; and Chapter 13 is voluntary repayment for individuals with regular income. For the purposes of this book, we will only be discussing Chapter 7 and Chapter 13.

In conjunction with your attorney, you will determine which Chapter is best for you. Depending on which Chapter you file, you will be assigned to either a Chapter 7 or a Chapter 13 trustee. Your attorney should be able to tell you exactly what questions the trustee will ask prior to the 341 meeting so you will be prepared but, in realty, there is nothing to prepare for, you simply tell the truth and everything will be fine.

The 341 meeting is called the meeting of creditors but in fact, it is rare that a creditor attends the meeting or asks any questions. In the rare situation where a creditor may appear, you should have been forewarned by your attorney. For most debts, like credit cards, medical bills, car loans, and mortgages, the creditors are well aware of the bankruptcy rules and are more concerned with not violating any federal bankruptcy laws then trying to recover from you or questioning you at the 341 meeting.

An example of when a creditor may appear is when it is an individual financially harmed and they do not know the law, and either cannot afford an attorney, or they want to look the debtor in the eye. This could be a homeowner who paid his contractor in full, but the contractor did not finish the job and filed for bankruptcy leaving the homeowner without a finished kitchen.

The 341 meeting takes place in an open room and not in a courtroom. There are several 341 meetings scheduled for each half hour and you sit and wait for your case to be called. The actual time speaking with the trustee varies based on your situation but on average, it is 4 to 8 minutes. Again, your attorney should let you know if your situation is outside "the norm." There should be NO surprises. Bankruptcy is black and white i.e., it follows set rules, and that is one of the reasons why I love it.

Most people are very nervous leading up to the 341 meeting and that is natural since you have never gone through this process before. I can tell you not to be nervous, but it is only natural. However, after the 341 meeting, most clients remark, "that's it?!" One client who had not been able to sleep well the night before turned to me and said, "I got gypped. All that worry for nothing." Occasionally, the trustee asks for follow-up documents or further clarification but for the most part, your involvement is over. You should not have to meet with the trustee again or face a judge.

The only other requirement when filing for bankruptcy protection is you must take two on-line classes; one before you file and the other after you have filed. The classes are intended to help with your budget and to increase your understanding of financial pitfalls and troubleshooting. I say bankruptcy "protection" because that is exactly what it is, protection from your creditors. The result is for you to receive a "discharge" from your debt. In a Chapter 7 case, you should receive a "discharge" in approximately 60 days after the 341 meeting. In a Chapter 13, you will receive a discharge after you have made all your Plan payments.

A discharge means that you are no longer liable for any debt that you had prior to filing for bankruptcy. Most people understand that the medical bills and credit card balances simply go away. No one pays them on your behalf, they are just written off. You can voluntarily re-pay a debt if you want to, but the creditor cannot reach out to you or pressure you in any way.

The one concept that is somewhat difficult to understand is what happens to your secured debt when you get a discharge. People often say I do not want to include my house or my car in the bankruptcy, but every creditor must be listed. So, once you get a discharge, you are voluntarily paying for your home and car. <u>If you pay, you keep your home and your car</u>. And just like before you filed, if you do not pay, then the creditor can foreclose on your home or repossess your car. Since the mortgage and car are secured loans, the creditor can take back the property if you do not pay, however, since you filed for bankruptcy, you no longer have a personal obligation which means the creditor cannot come back after you for any deficiency. You should discuss this process and the option of "re-affirming" your secured debt with your attorney before filing.

The process for filing bankruptcy as outlined in this Chapter is over-simplified but for most people it is a very straightforward easy process. Your attorney knows the technical aspects of filing and the laws and he or she should be able to advise you of any action that you took that violated bankruptcy laws or may result in your case being dismissed. Similarly, he or she should point out any debts that will not be discharged such as student loans, most taxes, domestic support obligations, and debts that you incurred due to fraud, theft, or injury to another. Remember, ask lots of questions and be honest with your attorney and everything will go smoothly.

CHAPTER 3
Chapter 7 and Chapter 13

If you are able to file Chapter 7, then that is the fastest and easiest way to go. It does not matter how much debt you have, what matters is that you cannot repay it and you are seeking relief and a fresh start. If your debt is consumer debt, then your income will be evaluated to determine if you qualify for Chapter 7; this is called "the means test." Periodically, the United States Trustee updates and publishes new IRS allowance and administrative tables which determine if your income is above median and if your expenses allow you to file Chapter 7. If your income is above median, then you and your attorney need to accurately fill out the means test. This is the most technical part of filing bankruptcy and why you should not try to file on your own.

As previously outlined, if you have below median income, then you can file Chapter 7. Approximately five weeks after you file, you will meet with the Chapter 7 trustee and 60 days after that, you will receive your discharge. Bing bang boom. However, if you have above median income, you may (or may not) have to file Chapter 13. The median income as of May 1, 2020 is based on family size and is listed in Addendum A. Even if the median changes, the change should not be drastic so the chart and Addendum A should give you a quick reference point if you are able to file Chapter 7. (The actual median income amounts change frequently so you should "Google it" to get the current median income.)

Although you do not receive a Chapter 7 discharge for approximately 3 months after you file, all collection activity pretty much stops on the day you file. Any and every creditor that is tied into the credit bureau is immediately notified that you filed. It goes on your credit report and they stop calling and sending notices. If they have taken you to court, then they must remove it from the court's docket. Bankruptcy is very powerful, and it works fast. Creditors do not want to violate federal bankruptcy laws.

Earlier, we discussed how if you want to keep your home or car, then you must continue to pay. The mortgage and car loans are secured debt so if you do not pay, then they can foreclose or repossess but they cannot come after you. For that reason, when you file, these secured creditors may (and will most likely) stop sending you bills and will stop taking automatic withdrawals because they do not want to violate the law by attempting to collect their debt from you. You can and should continue to send the monthly payments whether by mail, phone or electronically but (initially) they will stop sending the bills. Your account will be moved to the creditor's bankruptcy department to ensure that the strict bankruptcy rules are followed. Later, the creditor can re-send statements if they wish as long as it includes a bold disclosure statement similar to this: IF YOU FILED BANKRUPTCY, THEN THIS IS NOT AN ATTEMPT TO COLLECT A DEBT FROM YOU PERSONALLY.

Other than this change in collection procedure, Chapter 7 does nothing to your secured debt. If you are behind when you filed, then you are still behind, and you will have to repay the pre-petition arrears. If you want to set up a repayment schedule with your secured creditors, then you will have to file Chapter 13.

At your initial meeting with your attorney, you would have disclosed all your assets and your attorney would ensure that those assets are protected. There is a list of federal and state exemptions and your attorney will decide which exemptions are best for you so that before you decide to file, you will know whether all your assets are protected or not. If some asset is not protected then you can either surrender it to the Chapter 7 trustee or you can file Chapter 13 to, in essence, buy it back and keep it. For most people, everything will be protected but if you have too many toys like three Harley Davidsons in your driveway, then unless you want to surrender one or two of them, you should not file Chapter 7.

To recap, if you are qualified for Chapter 7 then go for it however if 1) you make too much money according to the means test; 2) you want to set up a repayment plan or modify a secured loan; or 3) if your assets exceed your exemptions (i.e., you have too many toys), then you need to file for Chapter 13 protection. The Federal and MA State exemptions as of May 1, 2020 are listed in Addendum B. You are not expected to understand the Statute Summary that is your attorney's job, but I wanted to provide a quick reference point in case you are curious.

If you decide to file Chapter 13, the process is basically the same as for Chapter 7. Your attorney electronically files your case and approximately 5 weeks later, you have your 341 meeting with the Chapter 13 trustee. The Chapter 13 trustee's approach is a little bit different because rather than looking to liquidate unprotected assets, she is looking at your budget to see if a Chapter 13 repayment plan is feasible for you and to ensure that all of your available income is paid into the Plan.

In Chapter 13, there is quite a bit of interplay between the trustee, your creditors, and your attorney before you arrive at a final Plan payment. You should have a good idea what your monthly Plan payment will be before you file, but the final amount depends on the exact arrearage owed to a secured creditor, any priority claims that exist such as taxes, and sometimes the dollar amount of unsecured claims. There is no set percentage that must be paid to your unsecured creditors and it can range from 0% to 100% depending on why you filed Chapter 13 in the first place.

One of the reasons that you would have to file Chapter 13, is if you make too much money. After entering all your income and secured expenses into "the means test," it will calculate how much "disposable income" that you have. If it says that you have $250 a month disposable income, then you must pay at least $250 a month for 60 months. The percentage or dividend is then based on how much unsecured debt that you have. You can never pay more than you owe, but in this example $250 x 60 months equals $15,000 so if you owe $30,000, you would be paying a 50% dividend.

A second reason for filing Chapter 13 would be to pay back a secured debt over time. For example, if you fell behind on your mortgage and your home was about to be foreclosed, then you could file bankruptcy to stop the foreclosure. Let's say you were $24,000 behind on your mortgage and there was an auction scheduled for May 1st. You could file Chapter 13 on April 30th and stop the foreclosure. At that point, you would be considered current on your mortgage and on May 1st, you would start making monthly payments directly to the mortgage company. Then you would repay the $24,000 arrearage to the trustee in equal monthly payments over the length of you Chapter 13 Plan which could be from 36 to 60 months depending on your budget.

There are many people who file Chapter 13 to stop the foreclosure, but they cannot afford to pay back the arrearage. Filing will stop the foreclosure but only for 2 to 5 months which could be just the time you need to get organized and move out or it could give you the time to apply for a loan modification. Some people know that they cannot afford their home, but they just want to stop the foreclosure and get more time in their home and that is understandable. However, there are strict rules against repeat filers and that is the one time you would need to go to court and answer to the judge. You should discuss these rules with your attorney.

The third reason to file Chapter 13 is if you have too many toys i.e., unprotected assets. So, if you did not have an exemption to protect that third Harley Davidson, then you could only keep it or protect it by "buying it back" through your Plan. If the Harley was worth $10,000, you would have to pay the trustee $10,000 (plus her 10% fee) in equal monthly payments over the next 36 to 60 months. You would keep the Harley and the trustee would distribute your Plan payments to your unsecured creditors.

Once again, this book presents an over-simplification of Chapter 13 and you and your attorney would need to determine the best course of action and how much you could afford to pay. Despite the variables, it is a math problem and that is part of the reason that I love bankruptcy. It is not based on emotions or compromises; it is what it is. This is how much you make or owe, and this is how much you must pay to keep that asset. You can either afford it or you cannot.

CHAPTER 4
Chapter 20

There is no formal Chapter 20 in bankruptcy however, it is often called Chapter 20 when a person files a Chapter 13 and then converts it to a Chapter 7. Similarly, if someone gets a discharge in Chapter 7, they could later file Chapter 13.

As I mentioned earlier, someone may file Chapter 13 to "buy time" to try to get a loan modification. If the only reason why they were in bankruptcy was because of their mortgage arrears, then if they get the modification, they could dismiss their case or convert to Chapter 7 to get a discharge of their unsecured debt.

If the person did not get a loan modification and could not afford to pay both their current mortgage and their pre-petition arrears i.e., the Chapter 13 payment, then they could convert to Chapter 7 to get both a discharge of their unsecured debt and to ensure they would not be responsible for any deficiency after the foreclosure auction. After the 2008 mortgage crisis (and maybe they will again after Covid- 19), the legislature passed laws to prevent the mortgage company from sending you a 1099 for any deficiency after the auction. However, this law is no longer in effect and that means that you would be responsible to pay the taxes on the deficiency if the mortgagee sent you a 1099.

For example, if you owe $400,000 to your mortgage company and they get $300,000 for it at auction, then you could get a 1099 for $100,000. That is like kicking you when you are down. However, by converting and getting a discharge in Chapter 7, you would not be personally responsible or liable for your home or the $100,000 deficiency; you would not have to pay taxes on the 1099.

Filing for Chapter 7 and then Chapter 13 is the second "Chapter 20" but it is less common. There are strict rules regarding how often you can file for bankruptcy protection. If you get a discharge in Chapter 7 then you are not eligible for another discharge in Chapter 7 for 8 years. However, if you get a discharge in Chapter 7 and then want to file Chapter 13, you would only have to wait 4 years.

However, let's say for example that you were current with your mortgage when you filed for Chapter 7 two years ago but then you were laid off and fell behind on your mortgage. While you are not eligible for another discharge, you could file Chapter 13 to get current on your mortgage and repay your arrearage over the next 36 to 60 months. The point is that you can use the bankruptcy laws in different ways to protect your assets and <u>it is your choice</u> (one of the reasons to love bankruptcy); you do not need the creditor's approval to file bankruptcy and to get your finances and your life back on track.

CHAPTER 5
Mortgage Companies, Foreclosures and Loan Modifications

I do not work for creditors or know all their rules; I work with homeowners and I have that perspective. In 2009, I filed for bankruptcy to stop a foreclosure on my home and for two and a half years, I fought with my mortgage company to try to get a loan modification. I called 110 times and spoke to 97 different representatives and I sent in my complete application package (over 32 pages) of required paperwork 18 times. Five times they "closed my file" and I later received a letter saying that I had been denied; three times because I did not make enough money and twice because I made too much money.

I ended up suing the mortgage company in US District Court and won at the summary judgment phase due to the "totality of the circumstances." They had mis-handled the process and lied to me. I had a client who had the same mortgage company and she got a loan modification while in bankruptcy but the mortgage company (the mortgagee) told me they could not give modifications if my arrears was being paid through the Chapter 13 plan. I had to dismiss my bankruptcy to be considered for the loan modification which exposed me to foreclosure once again.

I did eventually get the loan modification and a very small settlement amount, but it was not "a win". In 2007, my original loan was $315,000, but after paying my mortgage for almost two years and fighting with them another two years, my new principal balance in 2011 was $399,578.

It is true that the mortgagee has no obligation to give a loan modification, but they should be honest. In the end, I learned that the mortgage is king, and the laws are made to protect the king. The mortgage industry stabilizes our economy and if you do not pay your mortgage, then it is understandable that you will lose your home. But it seems to me that they could be more transparent in their practices and more lenient with repayment options.

There are lawyers who will fight the mortgage companies because of the predatory lending practices and because the foreclosure paperwork is incomplete (and some lawyers are very good at it) but for me, I feel that in the end, I will still have to pay my mortgage and I will probably owe a lot more than before I started. In other words, you may win the battle but lose the war.

The mortgage companies have gotten better with their loan modification procedures (thanks to all the state attorney generals who continue to sue them) but it is far from perfect or predicable. I have seen clients get a modification without even applying and I have seen people with a good income get denied. There are rules and guidelines that the mortgage companies follow depending on who owns your loan, but they never tell you the rules before you apply, only after they deny you.

Despite my pessimism, you should always apply for a loan modification before you file for bankruptcy. The most important piece of advice I can give you is to call immediately after you send in your loan modification package and ensure that they received a complete package.

If you do not verify the package is complete, then you may get a letter three weeks later saying that you are missing a bank statement (or something else is missing). Even though you sent the bank statement, you send another one, then three weeks later, you get another letter saying that the paystubs are outdated, and they need new ones. So, you send updated paystubs and now the bank statements are too old etc. **Avoid this circus and call right away to ensure your package is complete!** If they say something is missing when you call, then send it right away even if you know that you had already sent it. Then call again to ensure they got the paperwork and that your package is complete.

Some people are uncomfortable applying for a loan modification on their own and if that is you, then hire an attorney. However, I do not think the attorney makes much difference at all. The mortgage company is not afraid of your attorney, it just means you are paying someone else to fax or email your loan modification package. But again, if you are not good at paperwork and following up, then hire a lawyer or ask your perfectionist sister to help you (that is if you are willing to disclose your financial hardship to your judgmental sister).

Only a lawyer licensed in Massachusetts is legally allowed to charge you to help apply for a loan modification. There are many lay people or lawyers outside of MA who will make you promises and take your money, but you have very little legal recourse in those situations. Remember, no one can guarantee you that you will get a loan modification; it is the mortgage company's decision.

The other concern with trying to get a loan modification is the timing. The mortgage company is required to offer to review you for a modification before they foreclose. However, the problem is that they are often doing both at once; they are scheduling the foreclosure while they are reviewing your documents for a loan modification. They could deny you on Monday and foreclose on Tuesday. They could also approve you on Monday and cancel the auction scheduled for Tuesday. This can be the most stressful time of your life and the mortgage company doesn't seem to care that there are people's lives at stake here.

If you decide to file for Chapter 13 bankruptcy to set up a repayment plan (remember Chapter 7 cannot do that) and end the uncertainty or to keep your home after being denied a modification, then I would still recommend applying again one year after the previous denial. It is not bankruptcy law or any mortgage regulation, but I have found that sometimes the mortgage company would rather give you a modification then have you repaying them through the Chapter 13 Plan.

Mortgage companies like to have control and they lose some of that control when you file because now, they must hire a lawyer to follow the bankruptcy laws and rules accurately. Additionally, the accounting for the mortgage company becomes more difficult and can come under the scrutiny of your bankruptcy attorney.

The last item I want to mention is that if you act early in the foreclosure process then there is less pressure and your potential Chapter 13 payments will be more reasonable. The steps in the foreclosure process are normally an initial letter from the mortgage company saying they are starting the foreclosure process; this is when they contact their attorneys. Depending how busy the law office and the land court are, you might receive the next notice in any where from 2 to 6 months. The second Notice is the Servicemembers Civil Relief Act which has a 30-day response time. Again, depending on how backed up the land court is, the final Notice of an auction date could be another 4 to 7 months later.

The long process is good if you do not want your house but just want to live there for free while you save some money for an apartment. But if you want to keep your house, then the 6 to 14 month delay means that your arrearage has increased by

6 to 14 mortgage payments and your repayment Plan amount will be even higher than it was when the process started. You might have owed $20,000 when you got the first Notice but 12 months later at $1800 a month, you owe $41,600. So, in this example, your Plan payment has increased from $371 to $771 a month which is a lot of money in addition to your regular monthly mortgage payment.

CHAPTER 6
Bankruptcy and Divorce

If you are using bankruptcy and divorce in the same sentence, then your life is not going very well right now. Although both bankruptcy and divorce are things you never expected to do, they are a reality. Many couples argue over money and that can heighten the emotions leading up to divorce. One spouse is spending too much or not earning enough and often the person trying to handle the bills is frustrated and tries to handle the problem on their own and then it all blows up out of proportion when it is discovered that the bills or mortgage have not been paid.

Bankruptcy can help in the divorce process or it can cause extra headaches. First the upside; if you have excessive credit card debt, this is (usually) considered marital debt and rather than fighting over it, bankruptcy just makes it all go away. The "responsible" spouse may not like it, but it is a fact and can save fighting and legal fees.

The downside of bankruptcy during divorce is that it can complicate the divorce proceedings especially if your spouse's divorce lawyer does not understand bankruptcy or your bankruptcy lawyer does not understand divorce. It can get legal and complicated so I will not dig too deep; one of the purposes of divorce is to divide marital assets but now you will need the bankruptcy court's approval to divide the assets.

If you filed Chapter 13 bankruptcy together and then you filed for divorce, there could be a conflict of interest and you may both need to get your own bankruptcy attorney. For example, if you are behind on secured debt, then one spouse may not want to keep the asset while the other spouse is trying to keep the asset but cannot afford it without the other spouse's contribution into the Plan. I had one joint

Chapter 13 case where there was a major debt owed to the mother-in-law; guess who no longer wanted to pay.

If possible, the bankruptcy and divorce should be planned together because in addition to the transfer and division of marital debt and assets, your status as married or separated, and the number of claimed dependents can influence whether the marital home is protected and whether you can file Chapter 7 or whether you must file Chapter 13 and pay thousands of dollars over the next 5 years.

Even if you cannot agree in advance, the most important rule is to communicate with your spouse regarding the timing and effect of a bankruptcy. Your communication skills are probably not at their highest when you are contemplating divorce but it is a factor that can either ease the tension and financial burdens or it can make everything more complicated especially in a Chapter 13 which requires payments and thus financial "agreement" over the next 36 to 60 months.

CHAPTER 7

Bankruptcy Versus Debt Consolidation

I am a bankruptcy attorney, so I am bias but both bankruptcy and debt consolidation have their advantages and disadvantages. For anyone who can file Chapter 7, bankruptcy is faster, cheaper, and more complete than debt consolidation. For the equivalent of 3 to 5 debt consolidation payments, you could file Chapter 7 bankruptcy and guarantee that all you unsecured debt will be eliminated.

In a debt consolidation situation, the company takes your payment each month and then takes their agreed to percentage off the top. The credit cards do not get paid and that fact is reported to the credit bureaus. This happens each month until the debt consolidation company has enough money to pay the settlement amount to one of the credit cards who then reports the debt as "settled." Then they save up your money again until they can "settle" with the next card. All the missed payments and settled accounts hurt your credit score and there is no guarantee that all your cards will agree to settle. The cards can still take you to court even as the debt consolidation people negotiate on your behalf. Be sure to ask your debt consolidation company if they go to court for you and if they do, what is the extra fee?

The one group of people who may benefit from debt consolidation are those people who have only credit card (i.e., unsecured) debt but who make "too much money" to file Chapter 7. If you think you may make too much money and you may have to file Chapter 13, then you should talk to a bankruptcy attorney *for free* and find out what the means test calculation payment would be. Then you can compare the Chapter 13 payment to the debt consolidation payment and make an informed decision. Even if the debt consolidation payment is a bit higher, it still may be a better option because (in this scenario) Chapter 13 payments would be for a required 60 months and debt consolidation usually has a shorter payment schedule. But again, make sure the debt consolidation company can ensure that <u>all</u> your creditors will settle and not just some or most of them.

Please do NOT enter into a debt consolidation agreement if you are eligible for Chapter 7; debt consolidation does not "look better" or save your credit, and there is no guarantee that all your cards will negotiate and settle. If you are already in a debt consolidation program and you cannot afford it or the process is not working for you, then consult a bankruptcy attorney and explore that option.

CHAPTER 8

Bankruptcy's Effect on your Credit

In the last chapter, we noted how debt consolidation negatively affected your credit score by having months of missed payments and "settled" accounts. This is because one of the biggest factors in your credit score is your payment history. Just like gaining or losing weight, it does not happen overnight. The longer your credit score has been sliding down, the longer it will take to get it back up. On the other hand, if you currently have a great credit score, then you will take an initial hit on your credit score, but it can rebound just as quickly.

One of my clients had a score in the low 700's and was paying timely every month but her entire paycheck was eaten up every week. Then her score started to dip because she was using up most of her available credit. (The credit bureau likes to see a maximum of 30% available credit used.) She filed Chapter 7 bankruptcy and her score dropped to 623 but six months later, it was back to 719.

On the other hand, if your score is already in the low 600's and you are either paying the minimums or nothing at all, then filing bankruptcy will have minimal effect on your credit score. The bankruptcy does stay on your credit for over 8 years, but it is not an anchor; the problem is that you have no one reporting positively to the credit bureau on your behalf. If you want to rebuild your credit, then you need to get some company to start reporting "on-time" payments. One of the best ways to get positive reporting is by getting two secured credit cards as soon as you get your discharge. I also recommend you sign onto a free service such as credit karma; they give great advice on how to rebuild your credit and get your score up. If you are diligent, it is possible to buy a home in just two years after you have filed bankruptcy.

Talk to your bankruptcy attorney about secured credit cards and the effect bankruptcy will have on your credit but very often and more important, the most truthful realization is that RIGHT NOW you do not need credit, you need money in the bank. The credit card companies now must show on the statement how many years it would take to pay off the cards if you paid the minimums each month and did not charge any more items. Look at your card statements and I ask you, why would you pay 6 more years on a card you cannot use when instead you could file, eliminate that debt, and keep those "minimum payments" in your bank account for the next 6 years? Do not be afraid that you will no longer have that "emergency" credit card because in a short period of time, you will have the money in the bank so you can use your debit card and not go further into debt.

Please NEVER cash out your retirement account or refinance your house to pay off credit cards. Get rid of the devil credit cards and keep the full value of the assets you have worked so hard for. It will be hard, but you need to break the cycle, budget, say "no" to your needy cousin, and use cash or a debit card; you have lived under this pressure for too long.

CHAPTER 9
Do Not Feel Bad or Embarassed

No one wants to file bankruptcy, but no one wants to stress out about money every day either. You have made the best decisions that you can each day, but life still happens, and you slowly fall into the credit trap and you become unable to pay your bills. Do not be embarrassed; you have the legal right to file bankruptcy and it is your decision. Filing for bankruptcy is public record, but unless someone is specifically looking, no one will know.

You can blame yourself for bad money choices but what does that accomplish. And many times, it is not your fault. Some life event happened, and money became an issue. It could have been a divorce, a job layoff, a medical situation, a family member who needed money, or even those buy now and pay no interest for two years gimmicks. This is America and every commercial pushes you to buy, buy, buy. Retail therapy is a real thing, but it has its consequences.

Well, the gig is up. File bankruptcy and get a fresh start. Then going forward try to make smart choices and avoid buying on credit. It will not be an easy road, but on your own, you will never get out from under all that debt. In the case of a mortgage company that refuses to work with you or may even refuse to accept your monthly payment, you need to take control. It is your decision and your decision alone. Remember, this is why I love bankruptcy. There are no surprises and you will finally get a good night's sleep.

Credit card companies do not need your money, you do! Mortgage companies do not care if you lose your home, you do!

CHAPTER 10
Frequently Asked Questions

1) **Do I qualify for bankruptcy?**

   Read chapter 3, everyone qualifies for bankruptcy; it just depends what Chapter and if it will help you.

2) **I do not want to put my house and car into the bankruptcy, do I have to?**

   All your assets must be listed but as long as you pay for your house and car, then you keep them.

3) **Who pays the credit card debt?**

   No one. The multi-million-dollar credit card companies write it off (and probably get a tax break).

4) **Does it look better if I have been paying my credit cards all along?**

It does improve your credit score and makes it easier to rebuild your credit.

5) **Does debt consolidation look better than bankruptcy?**

No one is "looking." The effect on your credit score and your ability to pay is what matters; compare your options and decide which puts the most money into your pocket?

6) **Do I have to be behind on my credit cards to file?**

No.

7) **Do I have to be behind on my mortgage to get a loan modification?**

You must have a hardship and that usually means you missed some mortgage payments. Mortgage companies have gotten into trouble in the past so they will no longer tell you to fall behind in order to get a modification but if you are currently paying the monthly payment why should they modify your loan and give you a better rate? If you are current with your mortgage, apply to refinance the mortgage, not to modify it.

8) Can I use my credit cards while I am thinking of filing?

You are not supposed to use your cards when you are insolvent. So, if you know that you cannot pay even the minimum, then you should not keep using your cards. However, if you need your cards to buy gas and groceries and you are paying the minimums, then there will not be a problem with using them. The credit card companies have a right to go back 90 days, but the violations would have to be flagrant, like buying luxury items or taking cash advances. Plus to recoup any monies after you file, the credit cards would have to hire a lawyer and then they only look back 90 days, so it will most likely not be worth it for them to go after you.

9) **Can I keep my Kohl's card or some other credit card?**

Sorry, no. You must list all your liabilities and even if you did not list your Kohl's card, they would know when the bankruptcy hits your credit report and they would shut you off.

10) **If I file can I keep my house and car**

Yes. In many cases that is why you are filing, to keep your house and car and to keep more of your paycheck.

11) **How much does it cost to file bankruptcy?**

Every attorney sets his own fees so you should ask however Chapter 7 ranges from $1500 to $3000 and Chapter 13 ranges from $3,000 to $5,000. Many attorneys want the entire fee up front for Chapter 13, but the fee is so much higher than Chapter 7 because the attorney should be working for free over the next 36 to 60 months. Many people are unable to finish their 36- or 60-month Plan so see if you can get part of the fee put into the Plan and that would save you some up-front money. It is good to be price conscious, but bankruptcy is a big deal and it is more important to hire a knowledgeable attorney than to save a couple hundred bucks.

12) **I signed a form with Jordan's Furniture saying that their loan was secured by the furniture; will I be able to keep my living room set?**

They may try to get it back but unless they are willing to spend attorney fees that are equal to or more than the value of your two-year-old dinette, then good luck to them. If you no longer want that furniture, just give back; the security is on the furniture, but they cannot try to collect the money from you

13) **I have a car that I cannot afford, how can bankruptcy help with that?**

After you file, you can return the car no matter how much you owe, and they have no retribution against you.

14)   My car has been repossessed; can I get it back?

When your car gets repossessed, they give you time to buy it before they auction it off. If you file bankruptcy before that auction date, they must give it back and you can include the towing and storage fees in your bankruptcy. You will still need to make arrangements to get current with your car, but it will be easier to pay them back if you have your car and can get to work.

15)   The credit card got court approval to garnish my wages, what can I do?

If you file for bankruptcy protection, they must stop the wage garnishment. Often your payroll department is slow to act so if they garnish after you have filed, then the creditor must return all the money they took post-petition (i.e., after you filed).

16)   I am on social security; can the creditors do anything to me?

Yes and No. If you are asking this question, the credit cards must be harassing you (or your parent) and you want it to stop. You are unable to answer your phone because they call all the time and they have taken you to court. This is what they can do to you – harass and upset you. They cannot garnish your social security check so if you do not have a home that they can put a lien on, they cannot make you pay.

If your only income is social security, then you probably used your credit cards to supplement your fixed income. You might have used the cards because your car needed a repair or you wanted to buy your grandson a birthday present and now over the years, the balances have gotten too high to keep paying them rather than to eat. If you decide to file Chapter 7, all the credit cards go away.

However, in less than a year, the credit card companies will send you more offers. They know you are a good credit risk because you had paid for so long and you have the fixed income. You do not want to get buried in debt again, but it would be nice to have the security to have a bit of emergency credit available. *(This is one of the few situations where I, Doug, would encourage getting another card unless it is for the sole purpose of re-establishing your credit.)*.

CHAPTER 11
Things <u>Not To Do</u> Before You File

1) Do not try to hide any assets by transferring them to someone else.

2) Do not pay back a family member or other creditor (insider) to the exclusion of the other creditors.

3) Do not take cash out of your bank accounts or try to hide cash at home.

4) Do not buy any luxury items or take cash advances on your credit cards.

5) Do not lie to your attorney.

6) Do not wear socks with sandals. (Not bankruptcy law, just fashion sense.)

7) Do not take your name off someone's bank account, car title or deed.

There are strict rules about preferential treatment, paying family and insiders, and transferring assets without receiving money value in return. The trustee will do a search of your social security number and if he or she finds newly transferred or hidden assets, he can retrieve them and or you could be charged with federal crimes and be denied a discharge.

DEDICATION
To my Mom

I grew up on a budget; I did not necessarily want for anything, but we did not waste anything either. We were taught to appreciate what we had.

My mother would often bring a coat or other clothing to Goodwill and she would always put a five- or ten-dollar bill in one or two of the pockets. She wanted a person in need to find the money so they would have a little something extra in their pocket. She did this for years until one day, she forgot something and had to return to the store after she had made the donation. To her surprise, she found the workers going through all the pockets; she came home mortified.

Years later, I was laughing with my mom about this memory and she told me that, even after that day, she always kept putting money into the pockets. She had determined that maybe they checked the pockets so the clothing could be washed before it was given away or sold. But either way, most of the workers were volunteers so whether they kept the "tip", or they donated the money to the charity, she continued putting a little something into their pockets.

Thank you, mom; you were both generous and kind.

ADDENDUM A

Median Income based on family size in Massachusetts as of May 1, 2020

Family Size	Median Income
1	$67,119
2	$84,125
3	$108,130
4	$134,418
5	$143,418
6	$152,418

ADDENDUM B
Current Amounts for Federal Bankruptcy Exemptions

The amounts allowed under the federal bankruptcy exemptions are adjusted every three years on April 1 to reflect changes in the Consumer Price Index. The federal bankruptcy exemption figures listed in this article are the April 1, 2019 figures. The federal bankruptcy exemptions will be adjusted again on April 1, 2022.

If you are married and filing jointly, you can double all of the federal bankruptcy exemptions. For example, you may claim a homestead exemption of $50,300 (which is double the listed homestead exemption amount of $25,150). (11 U.S.C. § 522(d)(1).)

If a dollar amount doesn't accompany a listed piece of property, the entire value of the property is exempt.

All code references are to 11 U.S.C. (Title 11 of the United States Code).

Homestead

522(d)(1), (5) - Real property, including mobile homes and co-ops, or burial plots up to $25,150. The unused portion of the homestead exemption up to $12,575 can be used for other property.

Personal Property

522(d)(2) - Motor vehicle up to $4,000.

522(d)(3) - Animals, crops, clothing, appliances and furnishings, books, household goods, and musical instruments up to $625 per item, and up to $13,400 total.

522(d)(4) - Jewelry up to $1,700.

522(d)(9) - Health aids.

522(d)(11)(B) - Wrongful death recovery for a person you depended upon.

522(d)(11)(D) - Personal injury recovery up to $25,150 except for pain and suffering or for pecuniary loss.

522(d)(11)(E) - Lost earnings payments.

Pensions

522(b)(3)(C) - Tax exempt retirement accounts (including 401(k)s, 403(b)s, profit-sharing and money purchase plans, SEP and SIMPLE IRAs, and defined benefit plans).

522(b)(3)(C)(n) - IRAS and Roth IRAs to $1,362,800.

Public Benefits

522(d)(10)(A) - Public assistance, Social Security, Veteran's benefits, Unemployment Compensation.

522(d)(11)(A) - Crime victim's compensation.

Tools of Trade

522(d)(6) - Implements, books, and tools of the trade, up to $2,525.

Alimony and Child Support

522(d)(10)(D) - Alimony and child support needed for support.

Insurance

522(d)(7) - Unmatured life insurance policy except for credit insurance.

522(d)(8) - Life insurance policy with loan value up to $13,400.

522(d)(10)(C) - Disability, unemployment or illness benefits.

522(d)(11)(C) - Life insurance payments for a person you depended on, which you need for support.

Wildcard

522(d)(5) - $1,325 of any property, and the unused portion of homestead exemption up to $12,575.

Massachusetts State Exemptions chapter 235 section 34

1) Homestead

- Up to $500,000 in the principal residence if the debtor filed a Declaration of Homestead with the <u>Registry of Deeds</u>.
- Up to $125,000 if no Declaration of Homestead was filed with the Registry of Deeds.
- Up to $1,000,000 if the homeowner of the principal residence is disabled or over the age of 62, regardless of the Declaration requirement.
- Up to $2,500 in rent per month if the debtor rents the dwelling unit as the debtor's principal residence.
- Burial plots and tombs are exempted.

2) Equity in automobile

- Up to $7,500 in one motor vehicle used for personal transportation or employment.
- Up to $15,000 in one motor vehicle if the vehicle is owned or substantially owned

by a handicapped person or an elderly person.

3) Household furniture

- Up to $15,000 in necessary household furniture.

4) Personal property

- All necessary clothing and beds for the debtor and his/her family.
- One pew occupied by the debtor or the debtor's family in a house of worship.
- Two cows, two pigs, twelve sheep, and four tons of hay.
- Military uniforms.
- One heating unit.
- One computer and one television.
- Up to $2,500 in bank deposits.
- Up to $1,225 in jewelry.
- Up to $600 in food.
- Up to $500 in Bibles and books.
- Up to $500 per month for utilities.
- Up to $300 in one sewing machine in actual use.

5) Tools of the trade

- Up to $5,000 in tools, implements, and fixtures.
- Up to $5,000 in stock-in-trade.
- Up to $1,500 in fishing equipment if the equipment is used for business.

6) Insurance

- Fraternal benefit society benefits
- Life insurance policies to a dependent
- Up to $400 per week in disability insurance benefits.

7) Pensions

- <u>ERISA</u> qualified benefits needed for support
- State employees
- Public retirement benefits
- IRA's needed for support

8) Public benefits

- Unemployment
- <u>Workers compensation</u>
- Public assistance

- <u>Social security</u>
- Veteran's benefits
- Moving benefits for exercise of eminent domain

9) Alimony and child support

- Amount reasonably necessary for support of debtor and dependents.

10) Wildcard

- Up to $1,000 plus up to $5,000 in aggregate value of any unused amount in the automobile, household furniture, and tools of the trade exemptions. Can only be used on personal property.

www.ingramcontent.com/pod-product-compliance
Lightning Source LLC
Chambersburg PA
CBHW061622130726
47996CB00003B/1082